Schools

By Sally Hewitt
Photographs by Chris Fairclough

FRANKLIN WATTS
LONDON • SYDNEY

This edition 2004

Franklin Watts
96 Leonard Street
London EC2A 4XD

Franklin Watts Australia
45-51 Huntley Street
Alexandria
NSW 2015

Copyright © 2000 Franklin Watts

Editor: Samantha Armstrong
Consultant: Steven Watts, School of Education, University of Sunderland
Designer: Louise Snowdon
Photographs: Chris Fairclough

A CIP catalogue record for this book is
available from the British Library
Dewey Decimal Classification Number: 370

ISBN 0 7496 5203 9

Printed in Malaysia

Contents

From above

This is an aerial view of a school.
The photograph was taken from
an aeroplane flying above the school.

- What would you be able to see in an aerial photograph of your school?
- How would it be different from this one?

Look at the buildings around the school.

- What different kinds can you see?

The school is surrounded by plenty of space.

- How are the school grounds used?

At the school gates

Schools are busy places with children arriving in the morning and going home in the afternoon.

- How do you get to school?
- Do you have to cross any roads on the way?

Lollipop people stop traffic so that it is safe to cross the road. They wear bright yellow coats so drivers can see them clearly.

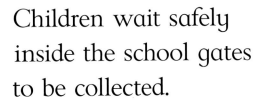

- What else makes it easy to see the lollipop person?

Children wait safely inside the school gates to be collected.

- Why is there a fence around the school?

Cars are not allowed to park outside the school.

- Why do you think it would be dangerous for cars to park near the school gates?

Village school

This school is in the middle of a village. It is surrounded by trees and grass.

• What do you think the children see on their way home?

Some schools are big and lots of children go to them. Other schools are much smaller.

• Do you think village schools are big or small? Why?

Old schools

This school is so old that your great-grandparents could have come here when they were young.

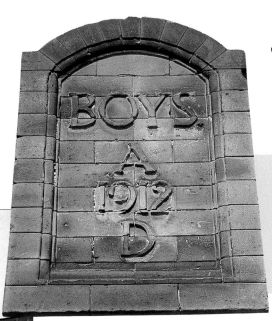

The date on the wall tells you when the school was built.

- Can you work out how many years old it is?
- Find out how old your school building is.

Look at the materials that have been used.

- How are they different from the materials used for a new building?
- Would you find decorated bricks like this at your school?

AIR RAID WARNING.
YELLOW & GREEN
FLASHING LIGHTS INDICATE
THAT AIR RAID WARNING
IS EXPECTED.

This notice was put up during the Second World War (over 50 years ago).

- Do you think your grandchildren will go to your school?

New schools

This new school building is in the shape of a big circus tent.

• Why do you think it was built in this shape?

This window is in the roof.

• Where are the windows in your classroom?

The school gate can only be opened if you press the right numbers on the lock.

• Who do you think knows the numbers and can let themselves in?

These children are looking over a painted wooden fence.

• What other kinds of materials have been used to build this school?

15

In the classroom

The teacher works with the children as they learn and play together in the classroom. The chairs and tables are just the right size for the children.

- Is your classroom like this one?
- How is it different?

Two children work together at the computer.

- Find the computer in the picture of the classroom.
- Why do you think it has been put there?

The children made this display to learn about growing tomatoes.

- What else could they use to help them learn about growing tomatoes?

Big windows let in plenty of light.

- How have the children used the windowsill?

Outdoor learning

There is a lot to learn outside the classroom. Some schools have gardens where the children learn about nature.

These children are looking at pond life.

• What outdoor places do you go to with your school?

This girl stays safe by keeping away from the edge of the pond.

• What else can you see in the big picture that keeps the children safe?

When you are out and about, it's a good idea to take notes to help you remember everything you see.

Behind the scenes

It's not only children who work hard at school. Some grown-ups work at school all day, before the children arrive and after they go home.

Teachers work together with the children.

• What do you think the teachers do to get ready for lessons?

The cleaner keeps the school clean and tidy.

• How could you help to make the cleaner's job easier?

There is plenty
to be done in the
school office.
The secretary checks
how the school's
money is spent.

The caretaker locks up
the school when everyone
has gone home.

• What other jobs does
the caretaker do?

Kitchen staff get the
school hall ready
for the children to
have lunch.

• Do you think the
kitchen staff work
at the school all day?

Games and sports

These children play games on the hard surface or on the grass sports field.

• Where do you think they play on a rainy day?

• Which sports do you play on grass and which do you play on a hard surface?

The hard surface and the grass have been marked out for games and races.

• Why do you think it is important to pick up rubbish on the sports field?

Secondary school

When children get older they go to a secondary school. Secondary schools are also called senior or upper schools. They are usually much bigger.

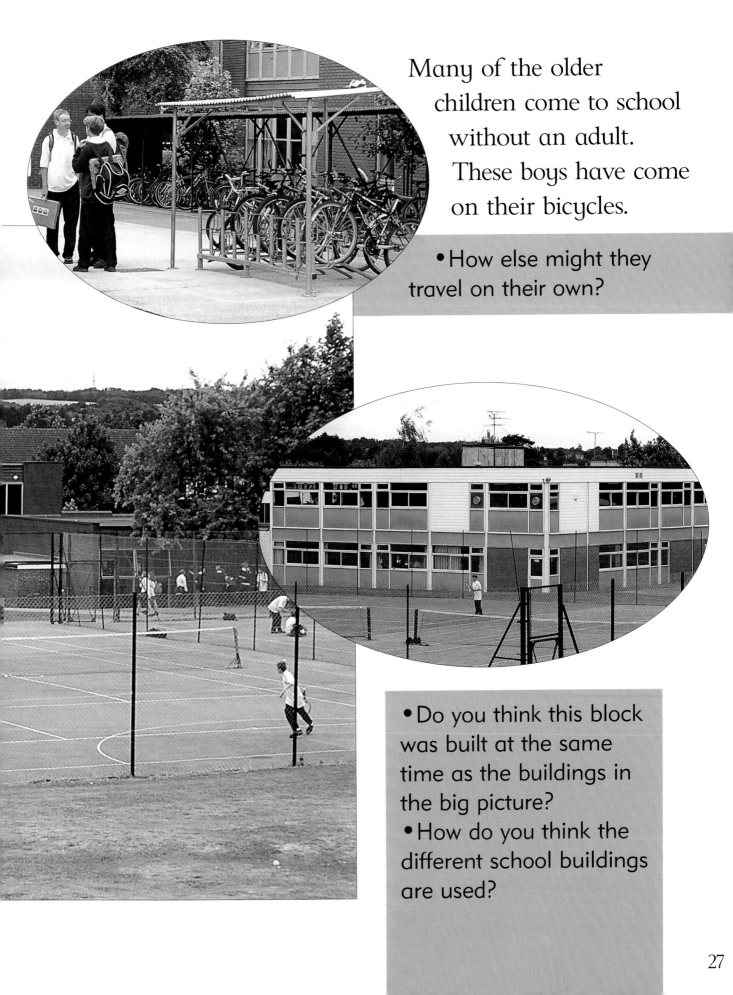

Many of the older children come to school without an adult. These boys have come on their bicycles.

- How else might they travel on their own?

- Do you think this block was built at the same time as the buildings in the big picture?
- How do you think the different school buildings are used?

Key words

Aerial view   an aerial view is what you see below you when you look down from above.

Building   buildings shelter people where they live and work. Schools, shops and houses are all different buildings.

Classroom   a classroom is a room in a school where people have their lessons.

Garden   a garden is where flowers, trees and grass are grown for people to enjoy. Gardens are usually next to a house or school.

Materials   things are made of materials. Brick, metal and wood are all kinds of building materials.

Mural   a mural is a large picture painted straight onto a wall.

Office   the school office is the room where school business is done. Visitors go to the school office first.

Playground   a playground outside a school or in a park is a place for children to play.

Town   a town is where people live and work. It is bigger than a village and smaller than a city.

Travel   you travel when you go from one place to another. Walking, going by bus or car are different ways to travel.

Village   a village is smaller than a town. Villages are usually in the countryside.

Get to know your school

1. Ask the children in your class how they get to school. Make a chart of the different ways they travel.
   - Which is the quickest?
   - Which is the slowest?
   - Which one do you think is best?

2. Draw a plan of your dream classroom.
   - Is it like your classroom at school?
   - How is it different?

3. Talk to the adults who work in your school. Find out what jobs they do every day.

4. • When was your school built?
   - How many different materials can you find in your school building?

5. Draw a map of your school playground. Mark on it the buildings, fences, walls, grass, the tarmac, any benches and the school gates.

6. Make a note of how your school is kept clean, tidy and welcoming.
   - What else could you do to make it attractive?

Index